PEOPLE AT
THE CENTER OF

THE
ENLIGHTENMENT

PEOPLE AT
THE CENTER OF

THE ENLIGHTENMENT

By GAIL B. STEWART

BLACKBIRCH PRESS

An imprint of Thomson Gale, a part of The Thomson Corporation

THOMSON

GALE

Detroit • New York • San Francisco • San Diego • New Haven, Conn.
Waterville, Maine • London • Munich

Photo credits: © Alinari Archives/CORBIS, 7; © Archivo Iconografico, S.A./CORBIS, cover, 8, 14, 24, 25, 30, 38, 43; Art Resource, NY, 10; © Bettmann/CORBIS, cover, 17, 21, 34, 35; © CORBIS, 27; Getty Images, 37; Giraudon/Art Resource, NY, cover, 15, 23; Image Select/Art Resource, NY, 20; Erich Lessing/Art Resource, NY, cover, 9, 19, 31; © Francis G. Mayer/CORBIS, 33; Nimatallah/Art Resource, NY, cover, 13; Réunion des Musées Nationaux, Art Resource, NY, 22, 26; © Leonard de Selva/CORBIS, 29; Tate Gallery, London/Art Resource, NY, 40, 41

LIBRARY OF CONGRESS CATALOGING-IN-PUBLICATION DATA

Stewart, Gail B., 1949–
  The Enlightenment / by Gail B. Stewart.
    p. cm. — (People at the center of)
  Includes bibliographical references and index.
  ISBN 1-56711-929-8 (hardcover : alk. paper)
Summary: Profiles prominent seventeenth- and eighteenth-century intellectuals—including scientists, philosophers, mathematicians and others—who, during the period known as the Enlightenment, emphasized the use of reason in their pursuit of truth.
  1. Enlightenment. 2. Europe—Intellectual life—18th century. 3. United States—Intellectual life—18th century. I. Title. II. Series.

B802.S74 2005
001'.09'033—dc22   2004022737

Contents

THE ENLIGHTENMENT

The Enlightenment was a time when intellectuals and philosophers began to emphasize the use of reason as the best way for people to learn truth. This period, which stretched from the early 1600s to the late 1700s, is sometimes referred to as the Age of Reason.

Reason was certainly not a new concept in the seventeenth century. After all, the ancient Greeks had described the power of reason in understanding the world thousands of years before. They developed the first ideas about nature and the laws of physical science. In the centuries since they lived, however, the Catholic Church had become a powerful force, and its leaders insisted that reason was valuable only as a way to understand God. Learning and reason had become only a means to seek divine truth.

Historians say that the Enlightenment grew out of an explosion of new knowledge in the sciences—astronomy, physics, natural science, and mathematics—that began in the early seventeenth century with the work of Italian scientist Galileo. Galileo disproved laws of matter and motion that dated back two thousand years to the ancient Greek philosopher Aristotle. He was followed by Isaac Newton, an English scientist, who explained in mathematical equations how gravity affected the planets and the Sun.

By daring to challenge ideas that had been accepted as true for thousands of years, Galileo, Newton, and other scientists of the seventeenth and eighteenth

Ancient Greek philosophers such as Plato (center left) and Socrates (center right) used reason to learn truths thousands of years before the Enlightenment.

centuries learned that the natural world operated by laws that could be measured, calculated, and explained. This new thinking inspired a number of European intellectuals to believe that all truth could be discovered in the same way. They began using reason and observation to take a new look at methods of government, education, economics, human rights, and a host of other topics.

These intellectuals believed that it was important to question and criticize other established authorities in the same way that Galileo and Newton had challenged long-held scientific beliefs. Many disagreed, for example, with the prevailing idea that kings and queens were ordained by God to rule. They criticized monarchies that were cruel and unresponsive to the people they ruled and called for new governments that would consider the well-being of all citizens, not just the wealthy relatives and associates of the king or queen.

Some Enlightenment thinkers questioned the authority of the Catholic Church. They criticized the church for its pronouncements of what people could and could

Galileo Galilei (right) dictates to a secretary. His work disproving Aristotle's laws of matter and motion launched the Enlightenment.

Galileo stands trial on charges of heresy for promoting ideas that went against Catholic Church teachings.

not believe. Galileo, for example, had angered the church when he contradicted official church teaching that the Earth was the center of the universe and that all stars and planets revolved around it. When Galileo's observations with his improved telescope proved that the Earth and planets actually revolved around the Sun, he was tried and convicted of heresy by a church inquisition. Such abuse by the church only increased the resolve of Enlightenment thinkers to promote reason over heavy-handed suppression of thought.

In challenging old authorities, Enlightenment thinkers arrived at fresh new ways of looking at things. Jean-Jacques Rousseau, one of the most famous writers of the time, suggested that education should be rethought. Instead of focusing on repetiton and memorization, he maintained, teachers would have better results if they found ways to make the curriculum interesting and meaningful to young students. Mary Wollstonecraft, a leading feminist of the Enlightenment, insisted that the human rights and liberty so valued by thinkers of the time should be extended to women, too. Philosopher Adam Smith suggested that an economy based on shared wealth for all workers was more just than one based on the exploitation by a strong nation of a weaker one.

America's forefathers sign the Declaration of Independence. The document contained phrases of Enlightenment philosophers.

The Enlightenment had profound effects on the times. Scientific discoveries, built on reason and observation, changed the way people viewed the world and their place in it. Perhaps the most enduring of its effects had to do with its revolutionary new ideas about human rights. Governments of the time were monarchies, in which power and wealth were held by the crown. Liberty, the ability to be self-governing, the freedom to say and write things without fear of being jailed were all ideas written about and discussed by Enlightenment thinkers.

Some of the same phrases used by philosophers of the Enlightenment—the pursuit of happiness, self-evident truths, and all men being created equal—were mentioned in the Declaration of Independence, the American colonies' announcement in 1776 of their desire for freedom from British rule. Twelve years later, these ideas were voiced again by the leaders of the French Revolution—and again and again as people sought political freedom from tyranny around the world.

GALILEO GALILEI

CHALLENGED ANCIENT SCIENTIFIC IDEAS

Galileo Galilei was born on February 15, 1564, in Pisa, Italy. As a young man, he entered college intending to be a doctor, but he changed his mind after a few years and began studying mathematics and physical science. He became a professor of mathematics at Padua University in Pisa in 1592.

Galileo believed it was necessary for any true scientist to observe and experiment, rather than to blindly follow theories that had never been proven. Much of the science taught in Galileo's day was based on the two-thousand-year-old theories of Aristotle, the ancient Greek philosopher. One such theory was that when two objects were dropped from the same height, the heavier one would fall faster than the lighter one. Galileo disproved this idea when he climbed the leaning tower of Pisa, dropped objects of various weights, and observed that they fell at the same rate.

Galileo made some spectacular contributions to the science of astronomy as well as physics. He improved a telescope, increasing its magnification by ten times. He was the first to see the craters of the Moon as well as the four moons of the planet Jupiter. He observed sunspots and discovered that the Milky Way was not a solid white band but was made up of countless individual stars.

Galileo's enthusiasm for using facts and observation created trouble for him, however. Another ancient Greek theory was that the Earth is the center of the universe, and that the Sun and other bodies revolve around the Earth. In the early 1500s, a Polish astronomer, Nicolaus Copernicus, had proposed that planets—including the Earth—revolve around the Sun. With his telescope, Galileo found evidence that Copernicus had been right. The Catholic Church was furious. With the power to dictate what could and could not be taught, church leaders banned the idea and warned Galileo not to pursue it further.

Galileo continued his support of Copernicus, however, and was convicted of heresy by a church trial in 1633 and sentenced to life in prison. He continued to work and write until his death on January 8, 1642. By proving that the Earth was not the center of the universe, in addition to his many other contributions to science, Galileo showed that laws can be proved and disproved with tests and observation. This idea became a key part of Enlightenment thinking.

Galileo Galilei believed that scientists must prove theories by observing and experimenting.

RENÉ DESCARTES

ADVOCATED REASON AND INTELLECT

René Descartes was born in La Haye, France, on March 31, 1596. From the time he began school, it was clear that he was a gifted student. His father had been a member of parliament and thought that his son might become a lawyer and follow him into government. Descartes excelled in mathematics and science, however, and was far more interested in the philosophical thought of the day than in politics.

In 1628, Descartes moved to the Netherlands. He had inherited money, so he was able to write and study without financial concerns. He surrounded himself with books and began a daily habit of meditation. Descartes accomplished a great deal during this time. He outlined a form of mathematics called analytical geometry, and he conducted a number of important experiments with lenses and light.

The most important of his contributions, however, was his revolutionary new method of thinking about humans and their place in the universe. Instead of looking at science and philosophy in terms of faith and religion, Descartes wanted to rely on reason and intellect. He urged intellectuals first to discard any preconceived ideas about the universe. Once they did, they could begin to view the world in purely rational terms—without involving religious doctrine or other long-held, unprovable ideas. Descartes believed that by using mathematical and scientific laws, people could find truths about the world on which everyone could agree. Insisting "Cogito, ergo sum" ("I think, therefore I am"), Descartes believed that the greatest tool in discovering real truths about the world was thought.

Descartes's intellectual method, which relied solely on reason rather than on the teachings of the Catholic Church, became popular among the great scientists and philosophers of the day. He became well known throughout Europe. In 1649 he accepted a request from Queen Christina of Sweden to join her court as a tutor. While in Stockholm, he caught pneumonia and died on February 11, 1650.

Opposite: René Descartes believed people should use reason and intellect to find truths about the world. Above: He became a tutor to Sweden's Queen Christina in 1649.

 John Locke

Advocated Government by People's Consent

John Locke was born in England on August 29, 1632. At the age of fifteen, he was admitted to Westminster School in London, a prestigious school that had what was called a scholastic curriculum—one that placed heavy emphasis on Latin, Greek, Hebrew, and memorization of the works of ancient Greek authors. While many of his classmates enjoyed the work, Locke felt it was useless and repetitive. He left England during the civil war there, choosing to live in the Netherlands, where he practiced medicine and wrote essays on his political and philosophical ideas.

When Locke returned to England in 1689, he began publishing essays on topics such as education, freedom of the press, and the nature of government. His best-known work was *An Essay on Human Understanding*, published in 1690. In this essay, he challenged many of the faults of scholastic education and the long-held ideas about how people learn. Ancient Greek philosopher Plato and others believed that people are born with certain knowledge, such as right and wrong, and that God exists. Locke disagreed, insisting that people's minds are like a blank slate when they are born. What people learn, he said, comes from experience and observation.

Locke also had controversial beliefs on the responsibility of government. For many centuries, political thinkers had maintained that kings and queens had a God-given right to rule their subjects. In an essay called *Two Treatises of Government*, Locke disagreed with the idea of a divine right of monarchs. He pointed out that kings often fought one another for control. Rather than divine right determining who ruled a nation, he said, it was often the one with the mightiest army who prevailed. Perhaps Locke's most important contribution to Enlightenment thinking was his insistence that government should exist only to protect and help people. Liberty and the freedom to own property were people's rights, he wrote, and government's main job was to protect those rights. Such ideas were extremely controversial in Locke's day, especially among nobility.

Locke's writings, especially those on government, were enthusiastically embraced by the founders of the United States. They used his ideas in both the Declaration of Independence and the U.S. Constitution. Locke died in Essex, England, on October 28, 1704.

John Locke's belief that governments should protect people and their property rights caused controversy among the nobility.

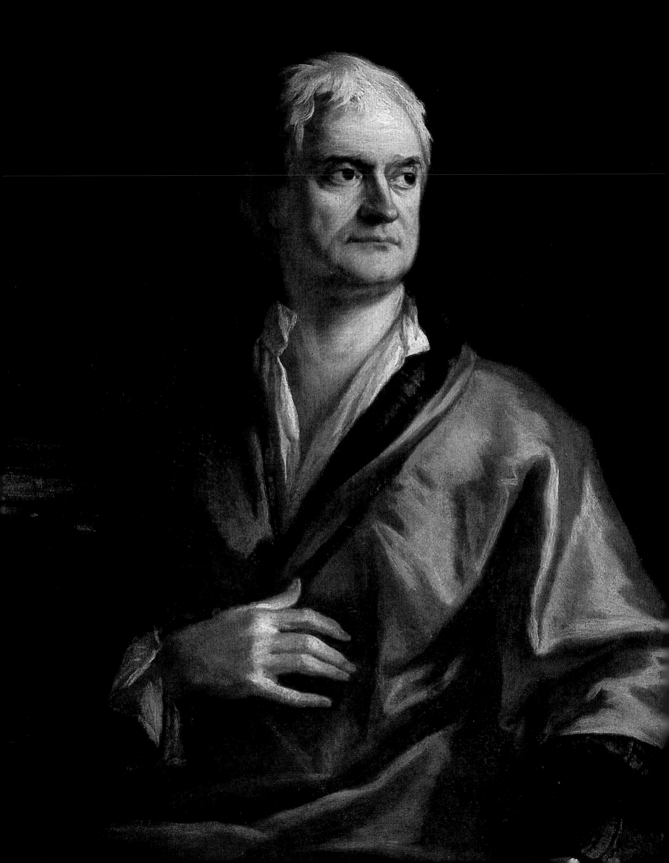

Sir Isaac Newton

Explained Gravity Using Mathematics

Isaac Newton was born on December 25, 1642, in Lincolnshire, England. His father, an illiterate farmer, had died three months earlier. Although he attended school, as a boy he was a poor student who was more interested in doodling designs for toys and little machines than in studying. He left school at age fourteen to help manage the family farm.

Newton was not cut out to be a farmer, however. He decided to enter Trinity College, part of Cambridge University, in 1661, and began studying science and mathematics. These subjects fascinated him and after graduating he became a mathematics professor at Cambridge.

In 1665, when an outbreak of the plague in England forced schools and colleges to close, Newton went back to Lincolnshire and continued his own research. During this time, he discovered an important law of gravity that affects the planets. Just as the Earth's gravity pulls objects toward it, the gravity of the Sun pulls the planets in their orbit. Newton's discoveries of the gravitational pull of bodies provided explanations of other phenomena, such as the Moon's effect on the oceans' tides. Newton published his findings, called *Philosophiae Naturalis Principia Mathematica* (*Mathematical Principles of Natural Philosophy*) in 1687. The *Principia*, as it is usually known, is regarded as one of the most important contributions in the history of science, for it laid the groundwork for much of modern physics. By proving that the Sun, planets, and the Moon move by the laws of mathematics, Newton inspired philosophers to look at the rest of the world using reason, too.

In addition to his discoveries about gravity, Newton also discovered some laws of optics, the study of light and vision. He passed a beam of white light through a prism of glass and found that he could separate the light into a rainbow of colors. This experiment explained that the color of an object is determined by the amount of light it can reflect. Using this new knowledge of light and the angles at which it is reflected, Newton built a new type of telescope, called the reflecting telescope.

In 1693, poor health forced Newton to retire from research. He was chosen Master of the British Royal Mint in 1699 and did important work by adding measures to make coins more difficult to counterfeit. Because of his groundbreaking scientific work, he was elected president of the prestigious Royal Society in 1703 and was reelected every year until his death in 1727.

Sir Isaac Newton's work in mathematics inspired philosophers to use reason in viewing the world.

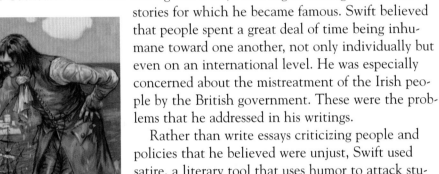

JONATHAN SWIFT

USED SATIRE TO CRITICIZE GOVERNMENT LEADERS

Jonathan Swift was born in Dublin, Ireland, on November 30, 1667. In 1689, he moved to England and worked as an assistant to William Temple, a diplomat and writer. He helped Temple prepare his memoirs for publication. During the ten years he spent in Temple's household, Swift had access to his employer's large personal library. He read hundreds of books on religion, philosophy, poetry, history, and science. During this time he also became a Protestant churchman.

Temple died in 1699, and Swift returned to Ireland, where he became dean of St. Patrick's Cathedral in Dublin. During this time, Swift began writing some of the stories for which he became famous. Swift believed that people spent a great deal of time being inhumane toward one another, not only individually but even on an international level. He was especially concerned about the mistreatment of the Irish people by the British government. These were the problems that he addressed in his writings.

Rather than write essays criticizing people and policies that he believed were unjust, Swift used satire, a literary tool that uses humor to attack stupidity or foolishness. *Gulliver's Travels*, Swift's most famous work, was published in 1726 and told the story of Lemuel Gulliver and his four voyages to strange lands. Although the book could be read as simply a comic adventure for young readers, an adult could see that Swift had created characters who displayed the same silly vanity and arrogance as politicians in their own time. By satirizing overbearing government leaders, Swift championed those people who opposed them. His work made him a key voice of the Enlightenment.

Throughout his life, Swift suffered from a disease of the inner ear that made him nauseated, dizzy, and at times, deaf. In 1740 he suffered a stroke that left him without memory and speech. He died in Dublin on October 19, 1745.

Above: Lemuel Gulliver arrives in one of four strange lands described in Swift's Gulliver's Travels.
Opposite: Jonathan Swift's satire gave support to people who opposed government leaders and policies.

MONTESQUIEU

ENVISIONED SEPARATION OF POWERS

Charles de Secondat was born on January 18, 1689, near Bordeaux, France. He was the oldest son of six children. In 1718, his uncle died and bequeathed him his title—the Baron of Montesquieu—which he used for the rest of his life.

Montesquieu studied law and moved to Paris in 1710, when the French Enlightenment was just beginning. He loved the city and especially enjoyed attending evening lectures on a variety of interesting topics, from the methods of the philosopher Descartes to Newton's groundbreaking scientific theories on gravity. The exciting discussions following the lectures encouraged him to write essays of his own on government and society. The first, called *The Persian Letters*, was published anonymously in 1721, for it was highly controversial. It ridiculed the phoniness and shallow behavior of many French nobles and religious leaders.

Montesquieu's most famous work was *The Spirit of the Laws*, which was published in 1748. In it, Montesquieu proposed that freedom can exist only in societies where everyone is free, and he condemned slavery and advocated a more humane treatment of prisoners. Montesquieu also wrote about the dangers of a government becoming too strong, and suggested that government should be separated into distinct departments, or branches. This was necessary, he felt, so that each branch could balance the power of the others. Montesquieu's idea of the separation of powers was used by James Madison and other framers of the U.S. Constitution when they divided the American government into the legislative, executive, and judicial branches.

Opposite: Montesquieu believed that all people must be free. Above: He moved to Paris at the beginning of the French Enlightenment and died there in 1755.

In the latter part of his life, Montesquieu traveled and continued to write. His philosophy of government—so influential to the ideal of democracy and free society—was widely discussed and debated in France and throughout the world. He died in Paris on February 10, 1755.

VOLTAIRE

François-Marie Arouet, who later went by the pen name Voltaire, was born in Paris on November 21, 1694. As a boy, he attended an excellent Jesuit school. Although Voltaire was a good student, he disliked the rigid teachings of the Jesuits. After seven years at the school, Voltaire came to resent the strictness of the Catholic Church.

By his teens, Voltaire had developed his own view of religion, which held that there was a God who created the world but who does not control the day-to-day affairs of people. This religious belief is known as deism and was widely held by the philosophers of the Enlightenment.

Although his father had hoped he would become a lawyer, Voltaire preferred writing. He had a quick wit, and the poetry and plays he wrote poked fun at well-known political and religious figures. In 1715, he wrote some satirical verses ridiculing a duke. Although the verses were written anonymously, Voltaire's style was easily recognizable. He was sent to prison and later exiled from Paris.

Opposite: Voltaire used reason in his writings to challenge authority. Above: His verses about a duke landed him in prison in 1715.

Voltaire wrote his first play, *Oedipus*, during his time in exile. The play was so successful that Voltaire was hailed as the greatest French playwright of the times. He continued writing plays and wrote poetry, history texts, philosophical essays, letters, and novels, as well. Historians say that Voltaire is important to the Enlightenment not because he came up with new ideas, but because he wrote about them in so many different ways. He targeted the church and government so often that the philosophies of the Enlightenment were well known to everyone. Because he was so prolific, and because his writings reflected his willingness to challenge authority by using reason, Voltaire is often considered the Enlightenment's chief spokesperson.

After living away from Paris for most of his life, Voltaire returned to the city in 1778, at the age of 83. He was able to see his last play, *Irene*, which was warmly received by audiences there. He died in the city of his birth on May 30, 1779.

CAROLUS LINNAEUS

CREATED A NEW SCIENTIFIC CLASSIFICATION SYSTEM

Carolus Linnaeus was born on May 23, 1707, in Rashult, Sweden. His father, a clergyman, was an enthusiastic gardener and passed the love of botany—the study of plants—on to his son. In 1727, Linnaeus enrolled in school, eager to learn medicine, botany, and other natural sciences.

Linnaeus graduated with a medical degree and an extensive background in natural science. He became a professor of botany and medicine at the University of Uppsala and dedicated himself to research. One of the things that most troubled Linnaeus was that there were so many new species of living things being discovered, but no accurate scientific system by which to organize them. The system in use was one created by the ancient Greek Aristotle two thousand years before. Aristotle had believed that all the plants and animals had already been discovered, and his system did not allow for new species to be added.

In 1735, Linnaeus created his own system, which he called *Systema Naturae*. He identified twelve thousand species of plants and animals, and he classified them with two names, rather than one. The first name was the family the living thing belonged to; the second was the individual species. Because of the use

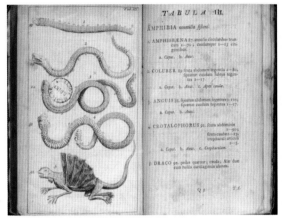

Opposite: Carolus Linnaeus's two-name system ended the confusion in classifying plants and animals. Above: Twelve editions of Linnaeus's Systema Naturae *were published during his lifetime.*

of two names, Linnaeus's system allowed scientists to be very specific when identifying a plant or animal. So that scientists did not have to learn a new language to use the system, Linnaeus used Latin words, because that was the international language of scientists.

Linnaeus and his students continued to name new species, and during his lifetime there were twelve editions of *Systema Naturae* published. His classification method, which is still in use today, successfully broke through the confusion of using a two-thousand-year-old system in an age in which scientists were rapidly discovering new species of living things. Linnaeus continued to do research and teach at the University of Uppsala until his death in 1778.

JEAN-JACQUES ROUSSEAU

ADVOCATED EMOTION OVER INTELLECT

Jean-Jacques Rousseau was born on June 28, 1712, in Geneva, Switzerland. When he was fifteen, he left Geneva and wandered through Europe, working at a series of jobs. In 1741, he went to Paris.

Paris was at the height of the Enlightenment when Rousseau arrived. There were lectures and intellectual conversations throughout the city, and Rousseau attended as many as he could. He met Denis Diderot, the rising French writer, and was hired to write several entries for Diderot's *Encyclopedia*. In 1749, Rousseau entered an essay contest on the topic of how morality was affected by the advances of science and art. He won, and when his essay was published, Rousseau became an instant celebrity.

Rousseau did not hold the same reverence for reason as did other philosophers of the Enlightenment. While he agreed with them that the authority of the Catholic Church and governments had been abused, he was not convinced that the solution to the world's problems lay in the use of science and reason. Rousseau's greatest contribution to Enlightenment thinking was his belief that the human heart—not intellect—provided more guidance than reason alone.

In an essay titled *Discourse on the Origin of Inequality*, Rousseau wrote that on their own, in a primitive setting, people are kind and have no need to hurt one another. Society creates selfishness, and as a result, people become aggressive and unkind. In another work titled *Emile*, he suggested that schools should change their methods for the good of their students. Rather than insist on rigid discipline and rote memorization, teachers should tailor their lessons to be appealing and interesting to children—and students will learn more easily. In his most famous work, *The Social Contract*, Rousseau explained that governments need to reflect the will of the people.

Rousseau continued writing until his death in 1778. His essays urging the need for human passion in government were inspirational to activists during the French Revolution, and his philosophy of education prompted the reform of schools in France and other nations.

French philosopher Jean-Jacques Rousseau believed that the human heart, more than intellect, should give guidance in solving the world's problems.

ENCYCLOPEDIST OF THE ENLIGHTENMENT

Denis Diderot was born on October 5, 1713, in Langres, a town in western France. As a young man, he attended Jesuit school for a time, but he changed direction at the University of Paris and studied philosophy and literature.

Although his native language was French, Diderot was fluent in English, too. After graduation, he found that he could earn a good living by translating important history and science books from English to French. He found many of the texts interesting and began writing essays in response to some of the works. Some of his first essays, published anonymously, came to the attention of Enlightenment thinkers, such as the French philosopher Voltaire, who praised his ideas. Although Diderot had always been a Catholic, he began to reject some of the church's views. In 1750, after writing an essay critical of the church, Diderot was arrested in Paris and jailed for three months for his radical ideas.

Opposite: Denis Diderot was jailed for his criticisms of the Catholic Church. Above: The seventeen volumes of Diderot's Encyclopedia *challenged conservative thinking.*

After he was released, Diderot began a project with French mathematician Jean Le Rond d'Alembert. They planned to translate into French a two-volume encyclopedia by a Scottish globe maker named Ephraim Chambers. Diderot decided to expand the project and make it a reference work including some of the most exciting, revolutionary thinking of the time—from philosophy and mathematics to literature and art. The *Encyclopedia* was published between 1751 and 1772, in seventeen volumes. It was highly controversial, because many of the articles challenged some of the conservative thinking of the time. In fact, after the early volumes were published, the official reaction from the French throne was very negative, for many of the articles criticized the government. As a result, d'Alembert became frightened and quit, leaving Diderot to continue on his own. The *Encyclopedia*, an official collection of world knowledge of the time, was the most important work of the Enlightenment.

After the *Encyclopedia* was complete, Diderot continued to write essays, plays, and satires. He died in Paris on July 31, 1784.

BENJAMIN FRANKLIN

AMERICAN SCIENTIST AND STATESMAN

Benjamin Franklin was born on January 17, 1706, in Boston. He ran away to Philadelphia when he was seventeen and became a printer. Although he had not attended school very long, Franklin had a quick mind and in his spare time taught himself science, math, and philosophy.

Franklin was a great admirer of Galileo and Newton, whose scientific discoveries were important to the Enlightenment philosophers. He, too, believed that reason and the scientific method would help people learn more about the natural laws of the universe. Franklin was an ingenious thinker, whose inventions included bifocal lenses and an improved stove that used a fraction of the fuel yet kept a home twice as warm as stoves commonly used in the eighteenth century.

The most famous of his experiments, however, was with electricity. In 1752, he flew a kite in a thunderstorm with the idea of learning whether lightning was actually electrical. The kite carried a pointed wire, and when lightning struck the kite, the resulting charge traveled down the string, where Franklin had fastened a metal key. The key sparked, proving that lightning was indeed made of electricity. Franklin's discovery made him a worldwide celebrity.

It was not only his scientific accomplishments that made him a giant during the Enlightenment. Like many philosophers of the day, Franklin believed strongly that human beings had natural rights to freedom and dignity. As a result of these beliefs, he worked hard for the success of the thirteen colonies in their quest for independence from England. He served as a diplomat in London, trying to work out a reasonable solution to the differences between the Americans and King George III. He was an active member of the Continental Congress in the colonies, formulating plans to collect money for the war effort. He served on the committee that drafted the Declaration of Independence. During the Revolutionary War, he served America as the ambassador to France, urging the French government to provide assistance and funds to the colonists.

Franklin returned to America in 1785. By this time he was eighty years old. Even so, he helped draft the first U.S. Constitution, urging cooperation and respect among the delegates. He died on April 17, 1790, revered as the key American of the Enlightenment—not only for his contributions to science, but for his work in making the revolutionary ideas of liberty and independence a reality.

Benjamin Franklin's scientific accomplishments and beliefs in human rights made him the key American in the Enlightenment.

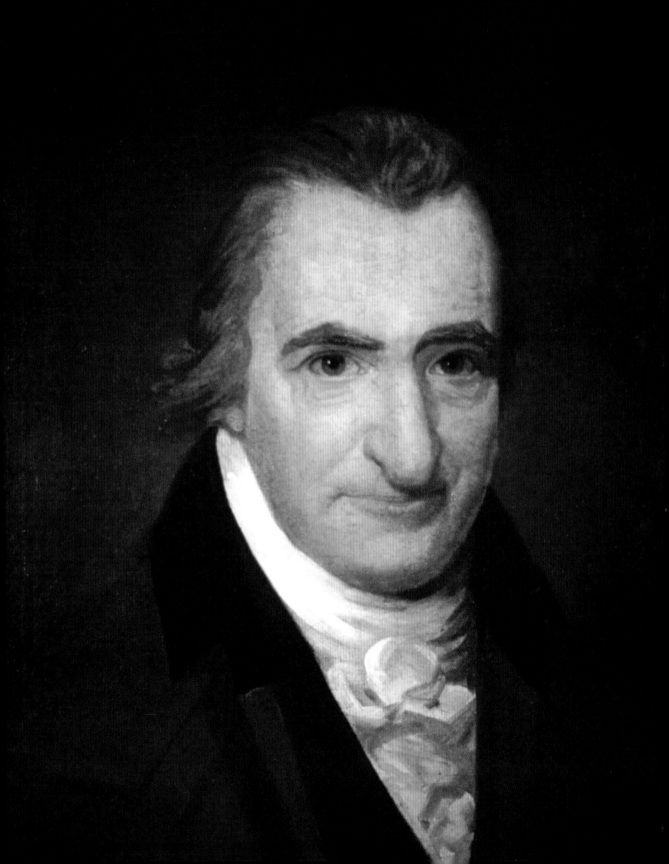

THOMAS PAINE

AUTHOR WHO ADVOCATED AMERICAN LIBERTY

Thomas Paine was born on January 29, 1737, in Norfolk, England. His father expected him to join his corset-making business, but Paine had no interest in it. Instead he liked to think about politics and read philosophical essays by Enlightenment writers and thinkers.

Paine began writing his own essays, calling for higher wages for working people in England. One of his essays caught the eye of American statesman and scientist Benjamin Franklin, who was in London trying to ease tensions between England and the American colonies. Franklin saw that Paine had talent and urged him to sail to America. There, Paine got a job as a writer for the new *Pennsylvania Magazine*.

Paine saw firsthand how strongly Americans felt about their freedom from the British throne. Drawing on the works of Rousseau, Locke, and other Enlightenment thinkers, Paine wrote *Common Sense*, a forty-two-page booklet criticizing King George III of England and applauding the voices in America that called for independence. *Common Sense* was a best seller—more than 120,000 copies were sold in twelve weeks. There were no new ideas or philosophies in the booklet. Its success was due to its plain, simple language. More than any other writer of the time, Paine inspired people in the colonies with his booklet defending American liberty and self-government.

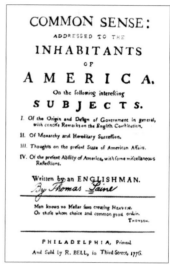

Opposite: Writer Thomas Paine inspired the American colonists to fight for freedom. Above: Paine's book Common Sense *criticized the English and applauded Americans who called for independence.*

After the Revolutionary War ended, Paine returned to England. When the French Revolution broke out in 1789, he supported it for many of the same reasons as he had supported the American fight for independence. He wrote a two-part book called *The Rights of Man*, which argued that if their government is unjust, people have a right to rise up in rebellion against it.

In 1794 Paine wrote *The Age of Reason*, in which he criticized organized religion. Like many other Enlightenment thinkers, Paine was a deist, believing that God existed but was not actively involved in the world. He returned to the United States in 1802 and died in New York on June 8, 1809.

ADAM SMITH

CRITICIZED PREVAILING ECONOMIC SYSTEMS

Adam Smith was born on June 5, 1723, in Kirkcaldy, Scotland. He entered Glasgow University at age fourteen, where he took classes in mathematics and philosophy. He won a scholarship to study mathematics at Oxford University in England. Later, when he returned to Scotland, Smith was hired to give lectures to various classes around the city. He was a good speaker and gave thoughtful answers to questions from his audiences.

In 1751, Smith was hired to teach at Glasgow University. He began writing essays on philosophy and economics. Smith's most famous work was a book called *The Wealth of Nations*, published in 1776. In it, Smith used many of the ideas of the philosophers of the Enlightenment to formulate his theory about why some nations were wealthy and others were not. He argued against the prevailing economic theory called mercantilism that was practiced in England and other European nations. Mercantilism encouraged the use of a nation's military to colonize other countries and accumulate their wealth—through mining, textiles, and so on.

Smith thought such a system was unjust, for it exploited other nations and too few people benefited from the rewards. Instead, he advocated a system that measures wealth not by its gold and silver, but by how productive its workers are. He believed that if all people were free to improve their own economic situations, everyone would benefit. Smith maintained that society should have a division of labor, so each person could work at what he or she did best. The more people who share wealth in a society, the freer and happier that society is. His idea that a nation's prosperity should be measured by the prosperity of its workers became the foundation of modern economic thinking.

The Wealth of Nations was a best seller soon after it was published. It attracted readers all over Europe. Even in the American colonies, founders such as Thomas Jefferson and Alexander Hamilton supported the ideas in Smith's book. Smith continued writing and lecturing after the success of *The Wealth of Nations*. He died in Scotland in 1790.

Adam Smith used the ideas of Enlightenment philosophers to develop a theory of why some countries were wealthy and others were not.

CATHERINE THE GREAT

DREAMED OF A RUSSIAN ENLIGHTENMENT

Born on April 21, 1729, in Stettin, Prussia (now part of Poland), Sophie was a German princess. She lived at a time when royal parents often arranged marriages for their children as a way to secure treaties between nations. At age fourteen, Sophie was taken to Russia by her mother, so that she could marry Grand Prince Peter, heir to the throne there. Before she married, Sophie became known by her Russian name, Catherine.

Catherine and Peter were not well suited. He suffered from mental problems and was not a faithful husband. Catherine did not enjoy being married, but she did have ambitions to be the empress, or ruler, of Russia. She had supporters within the Russian army, and when her husband succeeded to the throne in 1762, Catherine forced a takeover of the government. She ordered Peter to be imprisoned and was crowned empress.

Besides being ambitious, Catherine was intelligent. She enjoyed reading philosophical essays, especially those by the new intellectuals of the Enlightenment advocating liberty for all citizens. Motivated by her reading, she wrote *Instruction*, her plan to reform Russia. She built schools, universities, and medical clinics. She became a champion of human rights for all. She suggested that Russia could be a far better country if its economic and social systems could be changed. Under the old system, peasants worked as little more than slaves for wealthy noblemen, and had no rights in government. Catherine believed that farmers who owned their own land would work harder, and that would be good for the nation.

Catherine's ideas for Russia were groundbreaking, but her intentions to bring the Enlightenment to Russia proved fruitless. Catherine did not have the authority to make these sweeping changes. She had taken the throne by force, with the support of the army and some nobles. If she angered them by making too many changes, she would lose the throne. As a result, Catherine's reforms were only ideas, and she continued the old system of suppressing the peasants and favoring the wealthy noblemen. She remained in power until her death on November 6, 1796, in St. Petersburg, Russia.

Catherine the Great's efforts to bring Enlightenment ideas to Russia failed because she did not have the authority to make changes.

MARY WOLLSTONECRAFT

Mary Wollstonecraft was born in London on April 27, 1759. Her father was an alcoholic and was abusive toward her mother as well as his children. She attended school for several years, but her parents were unwilling to support any further education. In those days, most people considered education of girls beyond reading and writing a waste of time.

Wollstonecraft resented the fact that women had to be financially dependent on men to survive. Eighteenth-century society encouraged girls to marry and not to work outside the home. Despite such customs, Wollstonecraft left home at nineteen to earn her own income—first as a live-in assistant to an elderly widow and then as a superintendent in a school for girls. She believed that girls could grow up to contribute a great deal to society if only they were allowed the same educational opportunities that boys had. In 1787 she wrote an essay on this subject, called *Thoughts on the Education of Daughters*.

Finding that she enjoyed writing, Wollstonecraft began working on other essays. Her most famous was *A Vindication of the Rights of Woman*, published in 1792. In this work, Wollstonecraft became the sole Enlightenment voice for women. She criticized the long-held notion that women were morally and intellectually inferior to men. She insisted that women should have rights and privileges equal to those of men. After all, she noted, the key events of the age were the American Revolution and the ongoing French Revolution. Equality and liberty were the slogans of both, and she insisted that women deserved these rights as well as men.

Wollstonecraft had troubles in her personal life during this time. She and American businessman Gilbert Imlay had a daughter, Fanny. Shortly after the baby's birth, however, Imlay left Wollstonecraft. She eventually married William Godwin and gave birth to another daughter, Mary, in 1797. She developed blood poisoning soon after the delivery and died on September 10, 1797. Her daughter survived to become the author of the famous novel *Frankenstein*.

Opposite: Mary Wollstonecraft became the Enlightenment's voice for women by challenging ideas about women's inferiority.
Above: A young woman is married. Wollstonecraft insisted that women had more to offer society than marriage and childbearing.

1633	**Galileo is convicted of heresy by church inquisition.**
1687	**Isaac Newton publishes *Philosophiae Naturalis Principia Mathematica*, which details his findings about gravity.**
1690	**John Locke disputes the divine right of monarchs.**
1726	**Jonathan Swift publishes *Gulliver's Travels*, ridiculing English politicians.**
1748	**Montesquieu proposes a system of dividing government into branches, thereby separating power.**
1751	**First volume of the *Encyclopedia* is published by Denis Diderot.**
1752	**Benjamin Franklin becomes a worldwide celebrity because of his discovery of the nature of electricity.**
1762	**Catherine the Great takes the throne of Russia.**
January 1776	**Thomas Paine publishes *Common Sense*.**
July 1776	**American leaders send the Declaration of Independence to King George III.**
1792	**Mary Wollstonecraft calls for equal rights and education for women in her essay *A Vindication of the Rights of Woman*.**

Galileo Galilei demonstrates his telescope. Galileo was convicted of heresy in 1633 for his scientific ideas.